Empath
The 6 Types

April Stone

CONTENTS

INTRODUCTION TO EMPATHS

The modern world has brought forth a multitude of stress and difficulties. People often misunderstand one another's words and actions thus resulting in broken relationships. During these trying times, empathy is extremely rare. Yet, there are people who have the ability to appreciate and read people. Numerous people consider empathy as a gift.

This book is for people who wish to learn about empaths. Empaths are people with special gifts of absorbing energy. They can transform this energy for the benefit of others. If you suspect that you are empath, this book is just right for you. You will learn the basic concepts of being an empath, the different kinds of empaths, and the strengths and weaknesses of each type of empath.

On the other hand, this book can help you even if you are not an empath. If you know a person, who is an empath, it can help you learn more about empaths so that you can understand that person better. Moreover, this book is also for those people who desire to learn about empaths.

Why You Must Read this Book?

The people's view about empaths must change radically. Each individual must realize that energy is perceivable and real. Physical sensations and emotions are energy, which can transmit from one individual to another. Lastly, an individual can throw his energy to other people. This energy can stick and blend with other individuals. A person can also give away his energy.

There are empaths because they are helpful in

transforming emotional energy. They are in this world not to be just sponges that absorb the emotions and pains, but to be energy alchemists. Although they absorb energies of others, they do so to purify these energies in order for all creatures to continue to breathe and live.

Yet, people tell empaths that they are just vulnerable sponges. Due to the seeming disapproval of people, empaths try to suppress their gifts or use their powers wrongly. They twist energy without transforming it. At times, this twisting of energy is borne out of blind frustration.

An empath can extricate his own self from obsessing over another individual. He can do so by talking through the situation or shifting his attention. He may find it difficult to pull out, but the varied psychological means can be beneficial. However, an empath cannot shift his perspective, talk it through, and quit. Psychological approaches are ineffective because the energy of another person rests with the empath. Thus, it is important for the empath to undergo specific training.

The Difference between Trained and Untrained Empaths

An untrained empath can acquire the energy of another individual while attempting to help him. He has the self-care habits, inner beliefs, and the gift of clairsentience that he cannot handle adequately. On the other hand, a trained empath has the awareness and skills to have a neutral stance when dealing with the energy of another individual. He can still feel the other person's emotions, but he has the power to decide how these emotions will affect him.

A trained empath can be either altruistic or egotistical. An altruistic empath unselfishly helps to fill the desires or needs of others. On the other hand, an egotistical empath helps because he expects something in return. An untrained empath lies somewhere in between the two.

An egotistical empath is manipulative and selfish. He craves to be the center of everything. Normally, he has high Emotional Quotient. As such, he understands how other people's emotions. Therefore, he uses this understanding to pretend to help them, but with the expectation of receiving something in return. He is self-serving and a master of Empathic Manipulation.

Empathic manipulation can have various forms: dominance, humiliation, isolation, threats, intimidation, and denial and blame. For dominance, an abusive empath decides for the people around him. He treats them as if they are his possession. For humiliation, he will likely cause other people to feel dreadful about their own selves. He can do so by shaming, insults, public put-downs, and name-calling them.

For isolation, the empath tends to cut the person from the outside world so that this person can be more dependent on him. For threats, he uses threatening words in order to scare his victims so that they will not to leave or file charges against him. For intimidation, he can use tactics so that other people can submit to him. He does so to send a clear message that violent consequences can befall to them if they do not obey. For denial and blame, he blames everything on other people, things, and circumstances. He does not assume responsibility for his words and actions.

An untrained empath is another kind of empath who stays in the middle ground. He has undeveloped powers. He stays in the gray area because he is not aware that he is an empath. Furthermore, he does not know how to use his gifts. Therefore, he goes through life bearing the weight of the world clueless.

Stages of Being a Trained Empath

The Weighed Down Stage

An empath feels deficient and a burden. He wishes to eliminate this feeling. He needs to prove that he is tough, and not care too much about people, things, events, environments, and circumstances. He may not know that he is an empath.

The Fundamental Self-Care Stage

An empath moves to the next stage when he becomes aware of his need to rest and analyze things. He avoids over-stimulating environments and strives for peace with his sensitivity and "introversion". At this stage, he is aware of Highly Sensitive People concepts. He recognizes that he can be productive and perform better if he limits his stimulation.

The Energy Research Stage

At this stage, the empath starts to research about energy, and energy practices and tools. He selects meditation and visualization practices to help him stay rooted into the ground and cleanse his energy field. He may experiment with shielding, the attempt to block out other people's energy. Yet, he feels these practices are not enough.

The Empath Training Stage

At this stage, the empath takes advantage of an empath program where he can learn how to use his gifts and block other people's pain and stress. With an empath program, he can detect and feel definite improvements. He feels less overwhelmed with crowds, strengthens his knowledge about his gifts. Furthermore, he becomes extra comfortable with the kind of person that he is.

The Achieving Control Stage

Using the empath tools learned from the previous stage, the empath applies them to help others. He uses his unique gifts for other people. Yet, he understands that he has no obligation to do so. This way, he does not feel burdened. He already knows how not to absorb energies from people, things, environments, and circumstances.

The Developing Clarity Stage

By reprogramming the subconscious and using the empath tools, the empath is able to let go of intense emotions or energies that is not his. Although he still absorbs the energies around him, he is now aware of them. At this stage, he can help untrained empaths understand their gifts better.

The Empath as a Way of Life Stage

At this last stage, the empath has come to accept who he is. Although he may need to purge some energy from time to time, he can do so without difficulty. He continues to level up because he realizes that being an empath is a way of life.

THE EMOTIONAL EMPATH

What is an Emotional Empath?

An emotional empath is in-tune with his emotions. He is overly sensitive and cannot rationalize his feelings. Furthermore, he experiences the world intuitively. He is spiritually attuned, a natural giver, and a good listener. Moreover, he will stay with a person through thick and thin. He is a nurturer.

An emotional empath can sense a person's feelings. He has the ability to absorb positive energies. His body flourishes if he is around peace and love. Yet, he becomes exhausted if he is near negative feelings.

Therefore, he is a primary target of emotional vampires, who can ravage him through their rage or fear.

Emotional vampires are people who can drain the emotional energy of other people. They require constant attention and can be exhausting. They treat everything as a major crisis or event. They can elicit emotional responses from other people. Furthermore, emotional vampires have low self-esteem. They need excessive attention or validation, and tend to believe that nothing is their fault. Lastly, they do not recognize self-defeating patterns. They suck the emotions of emotional empaths.

Extreme negative energies can cause decrease in bone mass, a decline in metabolism, reduction in thyroid hormones, inability to concentrate, reduction in testosterone levels, and reduction in physical performance. They lead to weight loss and their bodies tend to slow down every non-survival function. Subconsciously, an emotional empath combats such negativities by overeating, thus causing him to gain weight.

In addition, the sensitivity of an emotional empath is overwhelming, especially in romantic relationships. Many emotional empaths remain single. They cannot settle their cohabitation requirements with their partner.

How to Identify an Emotional Empath

First, an emotional empath is extremely sensitive or overly emotional. People often come up to him to point it out because they can notice it easily.

Second, he feels perturbed if his friend is anxious. For example, a friend becomes anxious because he is going to speak at a conference the next day. An emotional empath becomes anxious himself if he is with his friend.

Third, an emotional empath feels hurt rather easily. This is because he is very sensitive to emotions.

Fourth, an emotional empath does not like big crowds because he can absorb all the negative emotions of every individual near him. He becomes exhausted, thus he needs to have his alone time to recharge.

Fifth, excessive talk, smells, or noise gets into an empath's nerve. An emotional empath often brings his car with him so that he can leave whenever he wants. He does so because he becomes weary of the negative energies he absorbs from people around him.

Sixth, if he is under emotional stress, he often overeats to cope with it. Overeating is his defense against negativity.

Lastly, he is afraid of intimate relationships because he often feels overwhelmed with them. He absorbs the emotions of his partner.

A person possessing at least three of the above characteristics is an emotional empath.

Strengths of an Emotional Empath

An emotional empath is attractive to other people. He is a trailblazer, powerful, sensitive, strong, and intuitive. In most cases, compared to her female counterpart, an empathic man experiences an arduous time because the society views sensitivity as too feminine or weak. Yet, he can balance both his masculinity and femininity to exemplify his full power.

An emotional empath can adapt to his emotions. He is profoundly sensitive and can feel everything. Yet, this is something challenging for him because society believes that a man does not cry. For him to succeed in controlling his emotions, he has to embrace his endowments and disregard the stereotypes. He needs to protect his energy in order to strengthen his empathy.

Furthermore, an emotional empath must realize he is one before he can be in charge of his emotions. He must know himself enough to express his needs. He has to improve his relationships and self-care to stay on top of empathy.

An emotional empath is a person with a big heart in helping other people. His sensitivity makes him attractively sensual, a great lover, and passionate. He is intuitive about the feelings and thoughts of people around him. Moreover, he can relate to the feelings of another person. He is in touch with his emotions and body. Lastly, he has an apparent sense of spirituality.

A female emotional empath has the same strengths as the man. Yet, she fosters chemistry and rapport better than his male counterpart does. She makes a good group leader, teacher, or counselor because she can sense the in the moment reactions of other people.

According to neuroscientists, the insula in the brain senses signals from the body. Thus, when a person is an empath, his brain mimics what the other person feels through the insula. For a female emotional empath, her brain tends to remain with

the other person's disturbing or upsetting feelin,
On the other hand, a male empath's brain tends to
focus on something else when such feelings arise in
the moment.

Weaknesses of an Emotional Empath

Loneliness

Emotional empaths are often lonely. They want a
romantic partner, but they remain single. On the
other hand, they may be in a relationship, but they
are often overwhelmed and fatigued. The reason is
that they are very intuitive and often absorb the
energy of their partner. Thus, they may shy away
from romantic relationships because they are afraid
of being overwhelmed. Emotional empaths, who do
not understand why they tend to avoid
relationships, will remain lonely forever. They want

companionship, but they are afraid.

There must be a redefinition of the conventional paradigm for copulating. Emotional empaths must be comfortable in a relationship. They have to assert their needs for personal space so they do not feel overwhelmed. This personal space can differ according to the empath's culture, upbringing, and situation. They will not gain emotional freedom unless they have their personal space.

Oftentimes, an emotional empath needs to sleep alone rather than with a partner. This is because energies combine during bedtime and can over stimulate an emotional empath. Lastly, an emotional empath needs to recoup lost energy. A brief escape from time to time can avoid emotional overload.

Other Weaknesses

An emotional empath absorbs the negativity in other people. He is like an emotional sponge. More likely, he is a wire without insulation, thus making him prone to fatigue, depression, and anxiety. He feels bound living with other people in the same house. Sometimes, he can have debilitating and chronic symptoms. Lastly, he finds it difficult boundaries with people who drain his energy. He can have various physical symptoms that conventional medical practitioners cannot diagnose completely.

Finding the Balance

Use the Intellect

An emotional empath who feels anxious must be able to employ logic and positive self-talk. He must assert within himself that he has no responsibility to assume the emotions of other people. He can love them sans the distress and anxiety.

Give Time to Emotional Decompression

An emotional empath must take mini breaks throughout the day to stretch, breath some fresh air, or take a short walk. Such activities will lessen the inordinate stimulation of going round-the-clock.

Apply Guerilla Meditation

To counteract emotional overload, the emotional empath must act swiftly to meditate. He must find a secluded place to relax. He can exhale the negative emotions while visualizing positive emotions penetrating him from head to toe.

Determine and Appreciate Empathic Needs

An empathic person must protect his sensitivities.

He can list down the top situations that make him emotionally stressed. Then, he can create a plan on how to deal with such situations.

THE PHYSICAL EMPATH

What is a Physical or Medical Empath?

A physical empath absorbs the symptoms of people around him. He cannot screen out and defend against the symptoms. To counter this, he must set healthy boundaries, protect and center himself, and ditch the energy of other individuals.

On the other hand, a medical empath is someone who feels sick when somebody nearby is sick. He can absorb the sicknesses and illnesses of other people. Yet, using his intuition, he can determine if a person has an illness. He is someone who can scan the inner body of a person and perceive any imbalance or illness.

An empathic illness is an illness that a physical empath exhibits symptoms, which are not his own. A physical empath may have agoraphobia, which is a psychiatric disorder caused by a fear of open areas, public places, or crowds. He can develop it because he absorbs the physical or medical symptoms of people around him.

At the onset, a physical empath may feel uncomfortable with the people. Then, he feels disturbed by them. The discomfort and agitation can get worse. Ultimately, he may avoid crowded places altogether. At some point, he will feel terrified of crowds. A physical empath may also experience chronic depression, pain, panic disorders, fatigue, and other mysterious illnesses, which react partially to medicines or psychotherapy

A medical empath is able to explain what is causing the ailment. Furthermore, he can expound the relation of the energy to an emotion. He can articulate the perceived information to the medical practitioner for further discussion and evaluation of potential treatments. Many medical empaths are medical doctors as well.

How to Identify a Physical or Medical Empath

An emotional empath and physical empath have similarities because they both absorb energies from other people. Yet, an emotional empath can absorb mostly emotions while the physical empath can absorb mostly pain or illness.

People sense that a person is a physical or medical empath if he is a hypochondriac or somebody who is extremely worried about his health. The physical empath talks incessantly about what ails him. Oftentimes, he seeks medical consultation, but the doctor cannot find anything wrong with him. Furthermore, he often has varied unexplained symptoms.

In addition, a physical empath avoids the crowds because he feels sick, tired, or uneasy with many people. This is because of his heightened empathy whenever he is with a crowd. He can absorb other people's symptoms, which makes him weak and sick. Thus, he frequently opts to stay at home. Other people may perceive him as an introvert.

Strengths of a Physical or Medical Empath

A physical empath is a repository of all the emotions and pains of other people. He is like the Russian Matryoshka doll, a doll nested inside a doll. Taking out the bigger dolls, one after the other will reveal the smallest doll inside and that smallest doll will be the physical empath. In close relationships, the physical empath is the sum total of the physical sensations of other people. This is because he can absorb the physical pain and emotions of people around him.

A physical empath is often a great provider and highly responsible. He is able to sense the physical needs of people close to him. He knows when a person needs material support so he shares his material blessings without the other person asking for them. Moreover, a physical empath can be the best provider of material goods. He can be the best father. She can be the best mother.

Yet, if the other partner is irresponsible, the physical empath can experience problems, including adrenal burnouts, illnesses, and fatigue. This because he can absorb the emotions of his partner. Thus, as much as possible, a physical empath must choose the right partner. He can also discuss it with his partner so that he can reduce the incidences of experiencing unnecessary problems.

Furthermore, a physical empath also absorbs physical sensations of other people like bodily pains, aches, and illnesses. He can be a caregiver because he can truly sense what is wrong with another individual. Thus, he can provide optimal care. Yet, he must take care not to become sick himself. He must learn to avoid overworking and overburdening. Many physical empaths can sense both material needs and physical sensations.

Weaknesses of a Physical or Medical Empath

A physical empath has a natural way of healing others through energy transfer. By sucking up the other person's energy, the empath is able to heal. He is like a dialysis machine, which runs the other individual's energy through his own system. He filters the pain through his own energy and body field.

Usually, the gall bladder/liver, bladder/kidneys, lungs, skin, or digestive tract filters the energy. An empath runs through disease, pain, or emotional issues of the person through his own filtering organs. The energy transfer is actually an exchange of energy. The high energy of the empath shifts to the other person while the lower energy moves to the empath, making him feel worse.

Unconsciously, numerous empaths do this. Thus, they are always sick. For instance, they have digestive ailments if they run other people's energy through their own digestive tract. They get anxious, sad, or depressed if they suck up other people's painful feelings.

Energy transfer works. An empath can make

another person feel better through it. Yet, energy transfer is a bad idea and an empath must learn how to heal other people without being sick himself.

How to Renounce Toxic Energy

Physical empathy is not bewildering. A physical empath can take on the pain of others, yet enjoy a richer, more insightful, and more comfortable life. Toxic energy need not affect his health.

Assess

First, the physical empath must ask determine if the emotion or symptom is his, someone else's, or both. If it is anger or fear, the emotion is his. The empath can resist the case of his emotion gently. He can do it on his own or seek professional help. If the emotion is someone else's, he needs to identify who is causing the emotion.

Move away

The physical empath must distance himself from the person causing the toxic energy. However, he need not move away completely. He can just allow a distance of at least 20 feet from that certain person. If he is in a public place, he can change seats so that he can keep the distance from the source of toxic energy.

Learn about sensitive points

Some body parts are more sensitive in absorbing stress. For instance, a physical empath's gut may be vulnerable. It can be the neck, the bladder, the head, or any other part of the body. At the start of symptoms, the empath can place his palm on the affected body part to send the love and kindness to the area. This way, he can relieve the discomfort. If there is chronic pain or depression, he can use the strategy every day to strengthen himself.

Concede to the breath

A physical empath can focus on his breathing if he thinks he is absorbing the symptoms of another individual. He must focus and connect to his power.

Engage in Guerilla Meditation

As soon as he realizes he is under physical or emotional distress, the physical empath must meditate immediately. He can do it anywhere to meditate. He has to focus on love and positivity to calm him.

Establish healthy boundaries and limits

Learning to say "no" is great for the physical empath because he needs to control the time he spends with other people, especially those stressful ones.

Envision protection

One of the best ways to counter toxic energy is to visualize white light surrounding the whole body. If he is with excessively toxic people, the physical empath can envision a ferocious black jaguar is protecting him against unnecessary energies.

What is a Geomantic Empath?

A geomantic empath is a person who can tune into the earth. He can sense any impending natural disaster. Subconsciously, he can read changes from the earth and energy signals. He knows if there is a coming flood or catastrophe.

Moreover, a geomantic empath is the same as an environmental empath or place empath. He attunes to the physical landscape. He feels happy or uncomfortable in some environmental situations or landscapes for no reason at all. He connects to some particular environments like churches, sacred stones, or groves. He absorbs the joy, fear, or sadness of the events that transpired in some locations. Furthermore, he is sensitive about a place's history.

A place empath is a person who can attune to the natural world. He grieves when people or circumstances damage it. He is aghast by the destroyed landscapes or cut trees. When he needs to recharge, he takes his rest in nature. Furthermore, he volunteers in environmental projects. He makes his surroundings beautiful and harmonious to make him happy.

How to Identify a Geomantic Empath

A medical practitioner may diagnose a person with panic or anxiety disorders. Yet, that patient may have symptoms correlated with being earth-sensitive or an earth empath. Modern science does not truly confirm earth sensitivity, thus it is just a pseudoscience or pure speculation. Yet, people who believe in it find ways to cope with it.

To determine if a person is a geomantic empath, he has to keep a health journal to write down the date, day, time, symptoms and duration of the symptoms. He also has to write down how he felt afterwards. The person must keep a journal for at least a month. Furthermore, he must be consistent in writing in his journal so that he can recognize and acknowledge the symptoms easily.

Next, the individual must monitor the natural catastrophes like floods, earthquakes, volcanic eruptions, etc. Then, he has to match the occurrences against his journal entries. After a month of close monitoring, he may be able to determine if he is a geomantic empath or not.

Normally, a geomantic empath experiences the symptoms about a day before the actual event and will only stop after it has finished. His anxiety ends as the event ends. He may suffer from nausea, vertigo, eye migraines, or energy drain. Moreover, his body experiences vibrations, mental confusion, emotional problems, and pressure in the ears. He has nightmares or dreams related to natural events, and mild physical pain. Lastly, he experiences an increase in the produced static electricity, and general shakiness.

Strengths of a Geomantic Empath

A geomantic empath finds it easier to live when he embraces his gift of foretelling a natural catastrophe. He can use it to serve his fellowmen by warning them of a possible flood, earthquake, volcanic eruption, etcetera so that they can prepare. Furthermore, Mother Earth is also calling him for assistance whenever he senses a possible catastrophe.

Each empath has his own way of assisting, and keeping his inner peace and balance. He can do once he discovers his gifts and learns how to use them. A geomantic empath may use crystals to keep balance the light-grid around the earth. He feels it if the greed is off balance.

On the other hand, another geomantic empath may meditate with Mother Earth or use her hands in the dirt of Mother Earth. He may feel the need to do so because if he does not, he gets extreme headaches. Yet, if he does, he experiences peace of mind and balance from within.

Weaknesses of a Geomantic Empath

A geomantic empath can experience numerous physical symptoms that are fleeting. He is able to predict a natural catastrophe because of symptoms like severe and sudden lower back pain, alternating feeling of high and low energy, abnormal headaches, itchy eyes, haziness or mental confusion. Furthermore, he can experience flu-like symptoms, loss of depth perception, sleeplessness, alternating increase and decrease in blood pressure, massive bone pain, nerve jolts, and eye socket migraines.

Moreover, a geomantic empath experiences short waves of nausea, burning in the bottom of the feet, stagger, tics, sudden problems with the ears, sudden loss of hearing for a short period, pressure in the ears, severe and sudden muscle spasms, dreams about natural catastrophes, and sudden itching or rashes.

How to Reduce Excessive Sensing

Spin

The geomantic empath has to stand straight while keeping his arms outstretched at his sides. He spins in place as he keeps right palm up and left palm down. If he becomes dizzy, he can use a chair to steady himself. He has to commit to perform more rotations gradually.

Ground

The empath must seek a grassy area. He must remove his shoes to feel Mother Earth as he raises both arms above his head. He must envisage energies entering his body and combining with energies from Mother Earth. Yet, some geomantic empaths have experienced extreme sensing after performing this.

Rattling

The geomantic empath can break up the energy using a Native American Rattle.

Gardening

An empath can immerse him in gardening to connect to Mother Earth.

Nature

Communing with nature is another way to reduce the impact of sensing. The geomantic empath can observe flowers, plants, and birds as he takes a walk in nature.

Walk mindfully

This strategy entails slow footstep so that the body can feel him in motion. Yet, the geomantic empath must walk with intention.

THE PLANT EMPATH

What is a Plant Empath?

A plant empath is a person with a close association to plants or flora species. He is able to sense the needs of plants, like where a particular plant wants to be and what plants it wants as a company.

For example, the plant empath is able to sense that a rose plant wants to be outside near the main entrance and it wants to be with other rose plants. He may have noticed that its leaves are starting to droop and so are its flowers when it was in another location in the garden. Therefore, he placed it near the door together with the other rose plants. After a few days, he has been able to notice the sudden change in the aura of the plant.

A plant empath can communicate with plants in a more intimate manner. In the essay "Roots of Consciousness" by Anil Ananthaswamy published in the New Scientist magazine, the author said that researchers found that plants are aware of other plants and their environment. Moreover, he said that plants could communicate what they perceive.

Botanists believe that plants are intelligent. For example, Anthony Trewavas of the University of Edinburg said that Cuscuta, a parasitic vine, behaved like a snake. This vine searches for a host then wraps itself around it. Yet, it even prefers one victim to another. For example, it chooses a tomato over wheat. Many people are actually plant empaths without them knowing it. They just have to be open about it so they can learn how to use their gift.

Intuitively, a plant empath understands plants or flora. He has a green thumb. He can put the right plant in its proper place in his home or garden. Oftentimes, his career involves caring for the plants in the parks, wild landscapes, or gardens. In some cases, a plant empath is able to talk to plants or trees and receive guidance from them.

Furthermore, a plant empath needs a continuous contact with plants and trees to strengthen him. He needs time to bond with them. He can just sit quietly by a plant or tree to attune with them.

How to Identify a Plant Empath

A plant empath is someone who concerns himself with the overall condition and the well-being of plants. He is someone who can interpret the plants' emotions. Furthermore, he can communicate with them. He knows their needs and tries his best to provide for such needs.

Moreover, a plant empath has stronger attachments to plants. More often than not, other people point it out. They notice that he has been extremely emotional and overly sensitive when it comes to plants. In short, he wears his heart on his sleeve. Other people can sense the feelings or cues that the plant empath may not even notice.

Even though the plants do not talk, the plant empath can sense their "emotions". He can absorb any negativity the plant may have. Plants affect him. For instance, cutting down of trees can be damaging for him while most people are not affected by it. A plant empath feels suffocated by crowds of people. Yet, he has been at peace when he is with plants and trees.

A plant empath enjoys an extremely vibrant inner life. He is imaginative, loving, and highly creative. He has a special relationship with his plants. He notices very delicate natural scents.

Strengths of a Plant Empath

A plant empath can connect with plant life by touching, speaking, or telepathic means. Plant life includes trees, vegetables, flowers, fruits, pollen, and the likes. A plant empath has the power to manipulate, shape, and create plants, including vines, moss, plants, and wood. He can help plants to grow healthy. At times, he can use these plants to heal people.

A plant empath can discern the general conditions and well-being of his natural setting and the immediate environment. He has a psychic sensitivity to nature, like forests, tundra, deserts, mountains, wetlands, and the likes. He is in agreement with his environment mentally, emotionally, and physically. This allows him to understand and perceive what is happening in nature. Furthermore, his interest is in ensuring that there is harmony with natural order.

There is a calm relief if the plant empath senses a tree naturally falling by itself. Yet, if the loggers cut the trees, the plant empath becomes agitated and will eventually feel sick. The natural death of nearby plants does not cause any unrest in a plant empath. Yet, if they cause the death of plants, men can perceive the plant empath as hostile to them.

Weaknesses of a Plant Empath

Other people will often reject a plant empath because of his belief in the life of plants. They may even think that he is crazy. Because of this, the plant empath can become stoic, if not outright unsympathetic, to other people. He does so after a prolonged interaction with plants.

A plant empath may not have actual power like the other types of empaths. Yet, it is possible to develop his skill or ability. The emotions of a plant empath are environment-related. If his immediate environment consists of plants and everything natural, he feels energetic and blissful. If not, he feels frantic, ineffective, anxious, or scared.

Apathy towards Other People

Apathy is a unique feeling because it is an "emotionless" feeling. Most people have encountered it at some point in their life. At present, it is now accepted science that before he can take meaningful action, an individual must have a compelling emotion about anything. Literally, apathy is the loss of feeling. A person has lost the motivation to act on anything.

For plant empaths, apathy arises from their strong connections to plants so much so that they become apathetic to their fellow human beings, especially when others dismiss them as lunatics. Yet, being apathetic, plant empaths also lose their faith not only with other people, but on themselves as well.

Stoic individuals lose the fundamental hope that personal fulfillment or happiness is possible. As such, they lose the emotional, physical, or mental energy to interact and accomplish tasks with other people. Yet, there are ways to reverse or resolve the apathy of plant empaths.

First, plant empaths must discover the source of their apathy and its underlying assumptions.

They must see themselves from another perspective in order to get past their shortcomings, transgression, or insensitivities.

Second, they need to move from being passive to becoming a problem solver. Instead of wallowing in apathy, they can list down how they can make their situation better.

Third, plant empaths need to initiate a conversation with other people. They can change their exercise routines or their diet. They need to search for ways to add novelty to their routines so that they do not remain apathetic.

Fourth, they can seek ways to challenge their apathy, like engage in activities that they found enjoyable in the past, but were not able to do now because they have become stoic.

Fifth, plant empaths can recall the times that they felt more alive and enthusiastic. Simple activities can reawaken a person to the simple joys of life.

Sixth, they can focus on a goal they are pursuing at the present. Given the present apathy plant empaths may feel, they can opt to take up a goal. They can focus their interest and attention in reengaging with life in a creative manner.

Seventh, plant empaths can seek professional therapy if they feel their apathy makes them depressed.

Overcoming Hostility towards Other People

Plant empaths may become hostile to other individuals. They do so if they feel rejected because of their closeness to plants and the environment. They may suffer from outbursts of hostility and rage because of this. Yet, they can restrain their intense feelings.

Plan empaths need to practice breathing exercises and remind themselves that they can manage the situation. They have to stop giving their aggressive feelings and thoughts to have power over them. If they feel threatened, they can reduce the threat by identifying the cause of their fear and weighing their options. If they feel angry, they can assess what makes them feel that way. They may feel hurt, disrespected, scorned, or rejected by others. If they feel frustrated, they can assess their needs and evaluate their options.

THE ANIMAL EMPATH

What is an Animal Empath?

An animal empath has an extraordinary ability to understand and recognize the mental and emotional state of an animal. He is able to interact with it. In some circumstances, he can even sway its behavior in a positive way.

In medieval times, people would have accused an animal empath of demonic possession, heresy, or witchcraft. They do so because of his ability to communicate with animals. They would view him in a negative way, especially if he expressed his views about animals that would run into conflict with the church dogma. They would punish him if they see him interacting or communicating with animals.

Yet, in some instances, people viewed the ability to empathize with animals as something miraculous. For example, Francis of Assisi had the ability to communicate with animals. People did not consider him as someone evil or practicing witchcraft. It is very probable that his saintliness reputation led people to believe his unusual ability as a sign of his holiness. In fact, the taming of the wolf of Gubbio by Francis of Assisi was extremely amazing that people viewed it as phenomenal, instead of vicious.

How to Identify an Animal Empath

First, an animal empath asserts that he and his pets understand each other. They know the each other's feelings and thoughts.

Second, he desires to know his pets' thoughts.

Third, an animal empath encounters bizarre animals, especially after seeing them on television or in a magazine.

Fourth, people, surrounding the animal empath, notice that he and his pets have begun to act and look alike.

Fifth, in some instances, an animal empath may even talk to bugs.

Sixth, he believes he sees a soul whenever he looks into the eyes of an animal.

Seventh, the animal empath likes to be with animals, instead of people. In fact, he likes them better than he likes human beings.

Eighth, he relates strongly to some kinds of animals like rabbits, cheetahs, butterflies, dogs, etc.

Ninth, an animal empath catches the attention of animals in an easy going manner, even if he does not want to. For example, a pet of another member of the family comes up to him as if he is its owner, even though he does not pay attention to it.

Tenth, he feels anxious, angry, or sad whenever he eats animals or animal products.

Strengths of an Animal Empath

An animal empath can understand the emotions or speech of different animals. Although uncommon, this ability can be a mental power or natural talent. An animal empath may be able to imitate animal sounds, like the mewing of a cat or the mooing of the cow. He may talk to animals using human or animal language. Moreover, he may even talk to them using telepathy.

Using telepathy, an animal empath can manipulate, read, and project an animal's thoughts. He can send information from his mind to the animal's mind. Furthermore, he can receive information from the animal's mind into his. At the basic level, telepathy allows the animal empath to sense or read the thoughts of animals. Because of this, an animal empath can interpret and/or communicate its emotions. By developing telepathic powers, an animal empath can control the minds of animals to do whatever he wants.

Weaknesses of an Animal Empath

Animal empathy does not apply to all animals. Thus, dangerous and aggressive animals can still attack an animal empath. His telepathic powers are no match to these animals. In addition, the animal empath may not be able to establish a bond with all animals. More often, he can only communicate with a particular animal or animal type. Moreover, if there is an extremely strong emphatic bond, he may even behave like an animal.

Various studies and books explored the relationships between food and mood. An animal empath may experience baffling depression and anxiety as he forges on the spiritual path of empath training. He may seek psychological help, read self-help books, follow the advice of psychics, and go on a gluten-free diet. Yet, he is still anxious and depressed.

Some animal empaths follow a strict vegetarian diet while some of them avoid animal meat, except fish. Yet, they cannot shake off their anxious and depressed feelings. They try calming activities or positive thinking exercises, but they still have the feeling of fear, sadness, and shame. An animal empath who is more in-tune with his gifts is likely to suffer the worst kind of feelings. Yes, changing his diet in a particular way can improve his symptoms tremendously.

Solution to the Feeling of Depression and Anxiety

Many empaths recognize the energy of food. If their diet and lifestyle are cleaner, they will perceive more energy. Therefore, vegetarians taking a spiritual path suffer worse than those people who are not conscious about their food intake. Untrained animal empaths may suffer inexplicable depression and/or anxiety. Some empaths many need to go on a strict raw vegan diet while others just need a minor change. Thus, it is important for an animal empath to experiment.

First, the animal empathy needs to remove all animal products in his diet for two days. Then, he reintroduces each product one by one. He must be mindful of his immediate reaction. In addition, he needs to monitor how he feels the succeeding two days. He can seek the help of other people around him if he is unsure of his behavior and mood, without telling them the reason why he is asking. If there is no difference in happiness, gratitude level, mood, energy, or animal response to the animal empath, he can stop his experiment.

Second, if there are obvious positive differences, an animal empath can bless and thank his food. Indigenous or Native American tribes still honor the spirit of the animal, even if they kill it for food. An animal empath can do the same. If he wants to continue eating animal products, he needs to acknowledge the sacrifice gently.

Third, for any negative symptom, the animal empath needs to check his present symptoms. He needs to assess the animal products that may be contributing to the problem. For instance, commercially raised chickens are extremely high-strung. An animal empathy may have bouts of insomnia and may become anxious after eating chicken. Reducing chicken consumption can be a first step to determine the cause.

Furthermore, avoiding dairy can open the gates of blessings. An animal empath can pick up the sadness of the mother cow because its milk will not go to its calf. Then, he punishes himself by denying legitimate abundance and blessing in order to alleviate his guilt feelings.

An animal empath who condemns himself privately must stop eating pork products. This is because pigs only possess intelligence like that of a 3-year-old kid. An animal empathy suffers from extremely low self-esteem after eating pork chops, ribs, bacon, sausage, ham, or any pork product.

Fourth, the animal empath can add more seeds, nuts, vegetables, and raw fruits in his diet. By doing so, he reduces his consumption of animal products automatically. Furthermore, the enzymes from these foods provide clarity and energy in dealing with many emotional influences.

THE INTUITIVE EMPATH

What is an Intuitive Empath or Claircognizant?

A claircognizant or intuitive empath is a person who has a higher spirit or self who puts the information into his mind. This information can be insights about situations and individuals. It can even be an idea. A claircognizant is an individual known for his keen sense of knowing that goes far beyond logic.

An intuitive empath is someone who solves problems and understands abstract concepts. He is extremely analytical. As a child, he is a know-it-all. Adults are in awe because he

's everything. Claircognizance is quite non, yet it is not as popular as ιudience or clairvoyance.

y people know psychics as individuals who clairvoyance and visions as gifts. They ιipate that these psychics have intuitions come from an amazing premonition or a ə from heaven. A few psychics can hear əs and see dead people.

gifted psychics can also obtain information ι less dramatic means like claircognizance. As such, people often dismiss claircognizance because they are expecting visions, fireworks, and visions. However, even though it is subtle, claircognizance, as a gift, is not powerless. A claircognizant can transmit information in writing through his power.

You are ready now to have the life you always wanted

Thoughts from claircognizance are different from a person's own thoughts. A person cannot generate claircognizant information. He can only observe and interpret it through his conscious mind. The claircognization information comes unexpectedly. The person's current thoughts have nothing to do with it.

Furthermore, thoughts protect a person from disappointment, embarrassment, or failure. Yet, claircognizance surpasses these fears. It comes from wisdom. Moreover, it will only be coherent in hindsight. It may require a leap of faith.

How to Identify a Claircognizant or Intuitive Empath

First, the intuitive empath knows things before they occur. He has a gut feeling that something will or will not work out. He knows the result, even before he hears the news. For example, he looks at a woman and realizes that she is pregnant. Unexpectedly, he thinks of an old friend. Then, the phone rings and the person on the other line is that friend.

Different intuitive empaths have different energetic responses to discern events. Some empaths may have goose bumps while others may experience a sudden pain in the stomach. It is up to a particular empath to identify his personal process of discernment.

Second, an intuitive empath tends to freak out on particular situations. This is because he is sensitive to energy. Crowded places, food, and loud noises can stimulate his sensory experiences. He often experiences heightened sensitivities in places that have had crowds of people. As such, he needs to train himself to search for blessings, instead of allowing fear to affect his energies.

Third, an intuitive empath can read body language. In fact, he is an expert at it. He can also identify energy patterns with other people. He sees the reason and the truth behind the person's lack of a harmonious energy with the world. However, to keep the peace and relationships, he has to transmit love amidst all the negativity, wrongdoings, and deception. An intuitive empath has the gift of intuition because he has to work on his spiritual life.

Fourth, an intuitive empath has clear visions. He has precise clarity of what he wants to manifest. He has the skills in transforming the vibrations and details into a visual format so that he is able to determine the messages behind such visions.

Fifth, the intuitive empath connects his soul to the souls of other people. He attracts the right individuals to support him. Furthermore, he supports and understands their experiences. He is the ideal counselor.

Furthermore, the intuitive empath is creative. He thinks out of the box. He can draw up different ways to solve a person's problem. He can even provide the advantages and disadvantages of each solution.

Sixth, the intuitive empath takes time to recharge in solitude. He does so that he can hone his gift and recalibrate his soul. The activity can be as simple as binge watching a TV series, walking alone in the park, or spending alone time in nature.

Seventh, the intuitive empath has the ability to create power. He masters his faith by taking charge of his life. He uses every tool available in his spiritual toolbox to ensure that he becomes a conscious creator.

Eighth, the intuitive empath can differentiate his feelings from the others. Many empaths assimilate the feelings of others into their own body and mind. The energies merge with their own, thereby polluting their inner self. More often, they become just like the others because they cannot distinguish their own emotions from the others.

However, the intuitive empath is in-tune with his inner self so he can distinguish his own emotions from the others. As such, any surrounding feelings or emotions have less influence on him. An intuitive empath can control how the others can affect him.

Ninth, an intuitive empath has a gift of letting other people understand how they feel and why they are feeling it. He can talk to others about their thoughts, worries, emotions, and dreams. He has a knack of putting into words what they cannot say.

Strengths of an Intuitive Empath

The intuitive empath is a unique person possessing highly developed spiritual, mental, emotional, and overall energetic sensitivities. He has unique deviations in his central nervous system. The configuration of his brain and nervous system is different from everyone else. Although science does not quantify and consider it, it is a view held by people who are self-aware of their capabilities.

Furthermore, an intuitive empath is extremely affectionate in expression and character. He is a great counselor and a listener. He likes to help other people and even puts their own needs first.

An intuitive empath can establish deep connections, yet he is unconscious about it. He may feel uncomfortable if there is an over-abundance of stimuli that he cannot confirm right away. He mends the situation immediately if he is in the middle of a disagreement. He may even avoid the disagreement all together. He prefers to solve a problem quickly and peacefully. Oftentimes, he resents his lack of self-control if says unkind words to other people to protect himself.

An intuitive empath exudes an authentic and warm compassion towards people and animals. He may not be conscious of it, but he is like a magnet that attracts individuals and pets. He is a beacon of light. Strangers find it easy to communicate with him about their life. An intuitive empath listens with compassionate understanding.

Weaknesses of an Intuitive Empath

One of the weaknesses of an intuitive empath is that he may not have a full understanding of the information he obtained. This is especially true for an untrained empath. The untrained empath does not have the necessary tools to comprehend the whole picture. Thus, he may feel disappointment, anxiety, and even depression.

Moreover, in some instances, an intuitive empath may not acquire the information he needs. He may have a question for his Higher Self. He uses the tools to obtain the information, yet he still does not obtain the information. This is especially true if he is trying to obtain personal information. In addition, some information is really unobtainable, limited, or difficult to find.

The intuitive empath can also experience sensory overload, which is a condition when at least one of the senses of his body experiences over-stimulation. Sensory overload can be a form of torture because the intuitive empath has an influx of information that his mind cannot wholly process at once.

Developing Claircognizance

A person can use automatic writing as a way to obtain claircognizant information. He gets a piece of paper and pen or opens a word document. Then, he asks a question to his higher self. He writes down anything that comes to mind. He has to ensure that his conscious mind does not meddle in the activity. His conscious mind cannot think about the information he is receiving.

Persistence is important in automatic writing. At first try, a person may get many pages of nonsense. Yet, if he persists, he can channel some clear insights that are full of wisdom. Keeping track of information makes it easier for a claircognizant to determine any emerging patterns in his intuitions or communications. This way he can understand his own ideas and thoughts and filter out things that originate from other sources.

Meditation can also help invite claircognizant information. It quiets and prepares the mind for receiving spontaneous intuitive information. A natural, balanced state of mind allows the claircognizant the ability to filter out stimulus received not from claircognizance. The claircognizant can discern his ideas and thoughts from those that came from an external force.

In most cases, claircognizance has been already at work. Yet, the person does not recognize its guidance. Being aware of his thoughts is an initial step. For instance, if he meets a new acquaintance or if someone tells him a story, he must be able to read between the lines to validate the claircognizance information.

CONCLUSION

Now that you have finished reading this book, you should have learned the following information about empaths:

Who is an Empath?

An empath is a gifted person who can absorb and transform energy for other people. He is able to purify the energies then give them away so that other creatures can breathe and live. He is not just a vulnerable sponge, as other people would like to believe. Yet, he can also suppress or use his powers wrongly, mostly out of frustration. Thus, an empath needs specific training to make use of his gifts properly.

The Emotional Empath

An emotional empath is extremely sensitive, yet he cannot understand why. He can sense the emotions of other people around him. He can absorb both positive and negative energies. His body exudes peace and love if he absorbs positive energies. On the other hand, he becomes exhausted if he absorbs negativities.

An emotional empath must learn to strike a balance. He must use his intellect so that he can use positive self-talk and logic. Moreover, he must set aside time for emotional decompression by taking mini breaks. He can meditate quickly as soon as he feels the emotional overload. Lastly, he must learn to protect his empathic gifts by planning how to deal with emotionally stressful situations.

The Physical or Medical Empath

A physical empath absorbs other people's symptoms. On the other hand, a medical empath feels sick if there is a sick person nearby. A physical empath can develop fear of crowds, open areas, or public places because he can absorb other people's symptoms. He may even be terrified of crowds because he experiences mysterious illnesses with them. The medical empath, however, can pinpoint the cause of the ailment, as well as explain the relationship between the energy and the emotion.

A physical empath or medical empath has to learn to use his gift without affecting his own body. He needs to assess first if the symptom or emotion is from another person or himself. Then, he must ensure to keep a distance of at least 20 feet away from the person causing the negative energy. Moreover, the physical empath must be aware of his sensitive points that absorb stresss that he can send kindness and love to the affected area. He must focus on his breathing in order to connect to his power. Furthermore, meditation can help him to stay calm in the midst of stressful situations. Lastly, he must establish limits and boundaries in his dealings with people.

The Geomantic Empath

A geomantic empath can sense an upcoming natural disaster. He can notice the Earth's changes, as well as its energy signals. Depending on the landscape or environment, he can feel uncomfortable or happy. He absorbs the emotions of the events that happened in certain places. Thus, he is sensitive to the history of the location.

Yet, a geomantic empath can feel physical symptoms if there is a possible natural catastrophe. He can reduce the excessive sensing by spinning in place with his arms outstretched. In addition, he can find a grassy area and feel the ground on barefoot while envisioning energies entering his body. He can also try using a Native American Rattle to break up the energy. Moreover, he can try gardening or communing with nature. Lastly, he can try mindful walking.

The Plant Empath

A plant empath is in-tune with the plants or flora species. He senses the needs of plants and communicates with them intimately. Many people refer to a plant empath as someone who has a green thumb. Many plant empaths work as gardeners, landscapers, and caretakers of plants in the parks. They find strength whenever they are in constant contact with the plants.

A plant empath may become unsympathetic or stoic to other people, especially if they reject his close affinity with plants. He may not have actual power, but he can develop his ability or skill to use his gift. If he becomes apathetic to people, he must find the source of this negative feeling and try to understand where it is coming from.

The Animal Empath

An animal empath is in-tune with the emotional and mental state of animals. He may even be able to command an animal to obey him. He is someone who understands the speech or emotions of animals. In some instances, he may use telepathy to communicate with them.

To counter negative energies, an animal empath can turn to a vegetarian diet. Yet, he may only need to make a minor diet change. He can experiment with not eating all animal products for the first two days. Then, he reintroduces the animal products one by one. If he notices a positive change, an animal empath can stop his experiment.

Yet, if he notices a negative symptom, the animal empath must assess which animal product is causing it. He needs to reduce his consumption of that animal product or eliminate it from his diet for good. Lastly, he can try adding raw fruits, nuts, vegetables, and seed because these foods lessen the desire to consume animal products. Moreover, the food enzymes offer energy and clarity about various emotional influences.

The Intuitive Empath or Claircognizant

The intuitive empath or claircognizant possesses a higher self or spirit that provides information in his mind. The insights can be about people, situations, and ideas. The intuitive empath is an abstract thinker and problem solver. He is someone with higher spiritual, emotional, mental, and general energetic sensitivities.

However, an intuitive empath may not understand all information he received. To the untrained empath, this will lead to depression, disappointment, and anxiety. On the other hand, an intuitive empath may obtain limited information. He may experience sensory overload, which can be tortuous.

What the Reader Can Do with His New Learning

People regard empaths negatively. Yet, this must change in a radical manner. Everyone must understand that energy is real and recognizable. It is possible to send energy to a person, in the same manner that it is also possible to receive energy from an individual. Furthermore, a person can force his energy into another. Energy can mix and stick with people. A person can also bestow his energy to another individual.

Empaths can change emotional energy. Yet, they are not sponges that suck symptoms and feelings. They can also become a medium for energy transformation. Moreover, they can purify the energy before transmitting it to other creatures for survival. Yet, people can be mean. They can show their disapproval of empaths. Some of these people even treat them as vulnerable sponges. Thus, empaths decide to censor their powers. Some empaths even use their powers negatively.

An empath, who reads this book, can find inspiration with his new learning. He can embrace his uniqueness so that he can use his special talents with energy for the benefit of other people. With the basic concepts discussed here, he can seek a deeper understanding of his gift. He may even undergo training to hone his skill.

On the other, a non-empath reader will find enlightenment after reading this book. If at the onset, he views an empath as a misfit, his enlightened self will now be able to embrace the uniqueness of the empath's personality. Furthermore, if he knows an empath, he will understand this person better.

APRIL STONE

Made in the USA
Middletown, DE
11 February 2018